Helping the Environment

Earth-Friendly Energy

by Nick Rebman

FOCUS READERS

BEACON

www.focusreaders.com

Focus Readers is distributed by North Star Editions:
sales@northstareditions.com | 888-417-0195

Produced for Focus Readers by Red Line Editorial.

Photographs ©: Shutterstock Images, cover, 1, 13, 14, 17, 22, 26, 29; iStockphoto, 4, 7, 19, 25; Pixabay, 8, 10; Tong Wu/TNS/Newscom, 20–21

Library of Congress Cataloging-in-Publication Data
Names: Rebman, Nick, author.
Title: Earth-friendly energy / by Nick Rebman.
Description: Lake Elmo, MN : Focus Readers, [2022] | Series: Helping the environment | Includes index. | Audience: Grades 2-3
Identifiers: LCCN 2021003743 (print) | LCCN 2021003744 (ebook) | ISBN 9781644938362 (hardcover) | ISBN 9781644938829 (paperback) | ISBN 9781644939284 (ebook) | ISBN 9781644939710 (pdf)
Subjects: LCSH: Renewable energy sources--Juvenile literature. | Fossil fuels--Environmental aspects--Juvenile literature.
Classification: LCC TJ808.2 .R43 2022 (print) | LCC TJ808.2 (ebook) | DDC 621.042--dc23
LC record available at https://lccn.loc.gov/2021003743
LC ebook record available at https://lccn.loc.gov/2021003744

Printed in the United States of America
Mankato, MN
082021

About the Author

Nick Rebman enjoys reading, drawing, and taking long walks with his dog. He lives in Minnesota.

Table of Contents

Chapter 1

Using Less Energy

The sun is shining. It's a hot day. A girl turns on a fan. It keeps her cool. And it uses much less energy than an air conditioner.

The girl opens the washing machine. She removes the clothes.

 Using a fan costs much less money than using an air conditioner.

But she does not put them in the dryer. Instead, she takes them outside. She hangs them on a line. In a few hours, the clothes are dry.

Many devices use energy even when they're not turned on. So, the girl and her mother buy a power strip. They plug their computer

Did You Know?

Some people hang **solar** lights outside to decorate their homes. Solar lights get their energy from the sun.

 A power strip can power several devices from one outlet.

and TV into it. They turn off the power strip at night. That way, their devices will not use energy.

Using less energy saves money. It is also good for the planet.

Chapter 2

Dirty Energy

People use refrigerators to keep food cold. They use water heaters to take warm showers. And they use air conditioners to stay cool. These machines help make people's lives more comfortable.

 One central air conditioning unit can use more energy than 15 refrigerators.

 In 2019, fossil fuels were the source of approximately 84 percent of the world's energy.

But they have a cost. They use large amounts of energy.

Energy can come from many different sources. However, most energy comes from **fossil fuels**. These fuels include coal, natural gas, and oil. People take fossil fuels out of the ground. This process can be harmful to nearby land and water. As a result, people and animals who live in the area can get sick.

Many power plants burn fossil fuels in order to create energy.

Did You Know?

In some places, people get coal by blowing off mountaintops. This process destroys forests. It also pollutes streams.

When fossil fuels burn, **greenhouse gases** go into the air. These gases are causing **climate change**.

Power plants pollute the air in other ways, too. This pollution does not affect everyone equally. That's because power plants are often near **low-income** neighborhoods.

Did You Know?

In the United States, more than 60 percent of electricity comes from fossil fuels.

 Black children in the United States are nearly twice as likely to have asthma as white children.

Power plants are also more common near Black communities. So, people in these areas breathe more polluted air. They tend to experience more health problems than people in other areas.

Chapter 3

Working on Solutions

People have come up with ways to use less energy. For instance, scientists have invented more **efficient** products. One example is LED light bulbs. They use much less energy than regular bulbs.

 An LED light bulb (left) lasts much longer than a regular bulb.

Other devices have become more efficient, too. Air conditioners are one example. Refrigerators and washing machines are others.

People have also found cleaner ways to make energy. These methods do not use fossil fuels. So, they do not create greenhouse gases. Solar power is one example.

Did You Know?

Using LED bulbs can help people save money on their energy bills.

 As of 2020, Honolulu, Hawaii, made the most solar power per person out of any US city.

Wind power is another clean source.

But these methods are not perfect.

Solar panels do not produce

energy when the sun is not shining.

Wind power cannot be produced when the wind isn't blowing. However, scientists are working on better batteries. They will help people store more energy.

Nuclear power can make huge amounts of energy. Nuclear power does not release greenhouse gases

Did You Know?

Billions of people cook with stoves that use wood, charcoal, or coal. Changing to Earth-friendly stoves can make a huge difference.

 In 2019, nuclear power provided nearly 20 percent of electricity in the United States.

into the air. But it does produce dangerous waste. For this reason, workers at power plants must store the waste safely.

Ocean Energy

Many people around the world do not have electricity. A girl in Florida wanted to help them. She knew that lots of people live near the ocean. The ocean's waves are always moving. This movement can turn **propellers**. So, the girl invented a new kind of propeller. It makes energy from the ocean's waves.

The girl hoped her invention could help in several ways. For example, it could power machines that make water cleaner. It could also power medical equipment.

Hannah Herbst helps other young female scientists.

Chapter 4

How to Help

To use less energy, you can make changes at home. For example, you can use LED bulbs. You can turn off lights when you're not in the room. And you can use a power strip. Try to turn it off at night.

 An adult can help you change your home's light bulbs safely.

Air conditioners use lots of energy. On hot days, try using a fan instead. Dryers use lots of energy, too. Instead, you can hang your clothes on a line.

To make a bigger difference, try to get large groups to make changes. Your school is one place to start.

Did You Know?

Everything you buy took energy to make. If you buy fewer things, you use less energy. So, try not to buy things you don't need.

 A US school tends to use one-quarter of its energy for lighting.

Find out what kinds of lights your school uses. Find out how the building is heated and cooled. Then, figure out who is in charge of those decisions. Ask that person to make the school more efficient.

In 2018, student protests started bringing more attention to climate change.

You can also find out how the electricity is made in your area.

Does it come from fossil fuels?

If so, write to the power company.

Ask the company for cleaner energy sources.

The biggest changes come from national laws. So, write to lawmakers. Ask for stronger laws on clean energy. If everyone gets involved, we can have a much cleaner future.

Did You Know?

Many people do not think about energy use. Talk to your friends and family. You can help people change their habits.

FOCUS ON
Earth-Friendly Energy

Write your answers on a separate piece of paper.

1. Write a paragraph that explains the main ideas of Chapter 4.

2. Nuclear power does not create greenhouse gases. But it creates dangerous waste. Do you think it is worth the risk? Why or why not?

3. What would help the most with clean energy?
   - **A.** buying an LED light bulb
   - **B.** creating stronger national laws
   - **C.** using a power strip

4. How would better batteries help people get cleaner energy?
   - **A.** Batteries could store nuclear waste.
   - **B.** Batteries could help create more wind.
   - **C.** Batteries could store solar power for use at night.

5. What does **sources** mean in this book?

*Energy can come from many different **sources**. However, most energy comes from fossil fuels.*

    A. places where something is moved to
    B. places where people do not live
    C. places where something comes from

6. What does **methods** mean in this book?

*People have also found cleaner ways to make energy. These **methods** do not use fossil fuels.*

    A. ways of doing things
    B. places that are clean
    C. amounts of fuel

Answer key on page 32.

Glossary

climate change
A human-caused global crisis involving long-term changes in Earth's temperature and weather patterns.

efficient
Able to do a job without using much energy.

fossil fuels
Energy sources that come from the remains of plants and animals that died long ago.

greenhouse gases
Gases in the air that trap heat from the sun.

low-income
Earning little pay.

nuclear
Having to do with parts of the tiny bits of matter called atoms.

propellers
Machines with spinning blades.

solar
Having to do with the sun.

To Learn More

BOOKS

Burling, Alexis. *Turning Poop into Power.* Minneapolis: Abdo Publishing, 2020.

Hirsch, Rebecca E. *Climate Change and Energy Technology*. Minneapolis: Lerner Publications, 2019.

Perdew, Laura. *Race to Renewable Energy*. Mankato, MN: The Child's World, 2019.

NOTE TO EDUCATORS

Visit **www.focusreaders.com** to find lesson plans, activities, links, and other resources related to this title.

Index

A
air conditioners, 5, 9,
16, 24

F
fossil fuels, 10–12, 16, 26

G
greenhouse gases, 12,
16, 18

L
lawmakers, 27
LED light bulbs,
15–16, 23

N
nuclear power, 18

P
pollution, 11–13
power companies, 26–27
power strips, 6–7, 23

R
refrigerators, 9, 16

S
schools, 24–25
solar power, 6, 16–17

W
wind power, 17–18